Forgive Me,
I Meant to Do It

Forgive Me, I Meant to Do It

False Apology Poems by
Gail Carson Levine

Illustrated by
Matthew Cordell

HARPER
An Imprint of HarperCollinsPublishers

"This Is Just to Say" by William Carlos Williams, from *The Collected Poems: Volume I, 1909–1939*, copyright © 1938 by New Directions Publishing Corp. Reprinted by permission of New Directions Publishing Corp.

Forgive Me, I Meant to Do It: False Apology Poems
Text copyright © 2012 by Gail Carson Levine
Illustrations copyright © 2012 by Matthew Cordell
For information address HarperCollins Children's Books, a division of HarperCollins Publishers, 10 East 53rd Street, New York, NY 10022.
www.harpercollinschildrens.com

Library of Congress Cataloging-in-Publication Data
Levine, Gail Carson.
  Forgive me, I meant to do it : false apology poems / by Gail Carson Levine ; illustrated by Matthew Cordell. — 1st ed.
    p. cm.
  ISBN 978-0-06-178725-6 (trade bdg.)
  ISBN 978-0-06-178726-3 (lib. bdg.)
  1. Children's poetry, American. 2. Humorous poetry, American. I. Title.
PS3562.E8965T47 2012   2009023978
811'.54—dc22   CIP
                                                                              AC

Typography by Martha Rago
12 13 14 15 16   LP/RRDC   10 9 8 7 6 5 4 3 2 1
❖
First Edition

To Susan Campbell Bartoletti,
who led me down the poetry path

Acknowledgments
To my poetry teachers, who may deny any connection to me
and this book—Kathleen Driskell, Molly Fisk, Sally Keith, Molly Peacock,
Vivian Shipley, and Nancy Willard

Contents

This Is Just to Say 51   This is Just to Say 52
This Is Just to Say 53 This Is
Just to Say 55 This Is
Just to Say 56   This Is Just to Say 58   This
Is Just to Say 59   This Is Just to Say
60 This Is Just to Say
61 This Is Just to Say
62 This Is Just to Say 64   This Is Just to Say 65
This Is Just to Say 67 This Is Just to Say 68
This Is Just to Say 70 This Is Just to Say 71 This
Is Just to Say 72 This Is
Just to Say 73 This Is Just to Say 74
This Is Just to Say 76 This Is Just to Say 78
This Is Just to Say 79
This Is Just to Say 80

This Is Just to Say

My bulldozer

has flattened

the thorny

hedge

which

you mistakenly

expected to sleep behind

until the prince came

Forgive me

I'm charging tourists

ten dollars

to visit the castle

This Is Just to Say

While you were buying

doll dresses

I sanded off

your Barbie's face

which

you constantly

patted

and praised

Forgive me

her beauty

was only

skin deep

This Is Just to Say

Dwarves

you snore

pick your noses

never take a bath

although

I always

encourage you

to be at your best

Forgive me

I'm making myself ugly

and leaving

with the witch

This Is Just to Say

You fell

and cracked

your skull

on the hill

where

I had carefully

placed

a banana peel

Forgive me

Jill

is now

my girlfriend

This Is Just to Say

If you have feet

I hope

you put on

slippers

when

my spaceship thunderously

shattered

your bedroom window

Forgive me

glass

is unknown

on my home planet

Introduction

―――

This Is Just to Say

Instead of at the beginning

I slipped

this introduction

in here

where

my editor excruciatingly loudly

screeched

it does not belong

Forgive me

I also shredded

her red pencil and stirred

the splinters into her tea

Blame my poems on the American poet William Carlos Williams, who lived from 1883 to 1963 and was a doctor as well as a poet. Here's his false apology poem:

This Is Just to Say

I have eaten

the plums

that were in

the icebox

and which

you were probably

saving

for breakfast

Forgive me

they were delicious

so sweet

and so cold

—William Carlos Williams

Imagine **his** wife coming downstairs in the morning after dreaming about those plums all night and waking up tasting them. Possibly she opens the icebox door (no refrigerators then) and finds a poem in the neatly washed-and-dried plum bowl. Maybe she laughs or maybe she goes for a very long walk or maybe she eats *his* breakfast and then writes her own false apology poem—

Which you can do too. Many poets have written them, following the form invented by William Carlos Williams. But don't even consider writing this kind of poem unless you can get yourself into a grouchy mood. You will be wasting your time.

If you do decide to write, your poems should be mean, or what's the point? Mine are, and William Carlos Williams's is too, in its subtle way. He's glad he got to those plums first!

You don't need a title, because William Carlos Williams has given you one, which can be repeated endlessly until your reader is completely sick of it. You also don't need a new ninth line, because that's always the same too: *Forgive me*. Notice that there are three stanzas, which you may agree are quite enough, and each stanza is four lines long, which you may think are four too many. The first stanza states the horrible offense. The second stanza describes the effect of the offense. The last stanza begins with Forgive me" and continues with the false apology, because the writer is not sorry at all. There is no punctuation (how nice!), and the beginning words of only the first and ninth lines need to be capitalized. The line beginnings and endings substitute for capital letters and punctuation. Normally, capitals and punctuation help the reader understand, so be careful to end your lines in a way that is very clear, unless you want to confuse your reader, which might be the wisest course.

Also, think about the rhythm of the lines. After you've cleared everyone out of the house, read your stanzas aloud to help you decide where to end a line. Funny poems are still poems.

You don't have to follow William Carlos Williams's form exactly if you don't want to. I haven't. You can add or subtract lines and stanzas. Or you can abandon the form completely and write false apology poems in your own cruel way.

For those of you who lack an ounce of mean and are reading this book only for research into the psychology of unpleasant people, you can write a real apology poem. However, even this will not be possible if you are too angelic to have anything to apologize for.

Whatever way you do it, have fun and save your poems!

—Gail Carson Levine

This Is Just to Say

I have eaten

your hot fudge

sundae

and the cherry on top

which

I thoughtfully

replaced

with anchovies

Forgive me

I gave three spoonfuls

of ice cream

to the cat

This Is Just to Say

I baked

a cottage

made all

of gingerbread

which

you and your sister

will be unable

to resist

Forgive me

I am hungry

and I prefer my food

young

This Is Just to Say

Tonight

we are eating

dinner

at Aunt Mildred's house

although

you will likely

throw up

when we get home

Forgive me

she made

her peppermint-spinach pudding

just for you

This Is Just to Say

I have chewed

through

the tall

beanstalk

which

you recently

stepped off

way up there

Forgive me

I think

I'm worth

more than five magic beans

This Is Just to Say

In your new prom dress

I danced

all night

with your boyfriend

who

accidentally

spilled grape juice

on the skirt

Forgive me

the stain

is almost

too small to see

This Is Just to Say

I convinced
Cupid
to pair you
with a warthog

whom
you will eternally
cherish
and love

Forgive me
warthogs
are very
affectionate

This Is Just to Say

The sharp teeth

the fur all over your face

and your new tail

are family traits

which

are charmingly

displayed in the portraits

hanging in the den

Forgive us

we should have

told you

sooner

This Is Just to Say

A single rose

adorned the table

while I breakfasted

on your daughter

which

proves regrettably

that I am

just a beast

Forgive me

please send

her sisters

by the next coach

This Is Just to Say

I recieved

my Joon

report

card

which

says I'm definitly

gonna be left

way back

Forgive me

the kids

in my new class

ain't been born yet

This Is Just to Say

I found
an old lamp
and called forth
a genie

who
is busily
granting
my wishes

Forgive me
time-out and *grounded*
and other unpleasant phrases
can no longer be uttered

This Is Just to Say

I have cast
a magic spell

on Louie
the bully

which
will soon
turn him
into a fly

Forgive me
my fly swatter
is already

ready

This Is Just to Say

I swiped

your lucky

baseball

cap

which

made you tragically

lose

the state playoff

Forgive me

the cap

keeps the sun

out of my eyes

This Is Just to Say

Spreading

across your skin

is an itchy

blistery rash

which

was deliberately

caused by yours truly

planting poison ivy on your lawn

Forgive me

next time

pay me

for mowing

This Is Just to Say

Ahead of you

you should see

a track

switch

which

will certainly

startle

and confuse you

Forgive me

you think

you can

but you can't

This Is Just to Say

I have shortened

my nose

with your saw

because

honestly

telling lies

is so much fun

Forgive me

I don't care

about becoming

a real boy

This Is Just to Say

You may be jumping around

and skipping

pages

in this book

which

I actually

spent ten years

arranging

Forgive me

I put the curse of the mummy

on anyone

who reads out of order

FLIP
THIP
FLIP
THIP

This Is Just to Say

To get my crimes

off my chest

I broke

into the cemetery

where

I confessed

to the bones

and the tombstones

Forgive me

dead men

tell

no tales

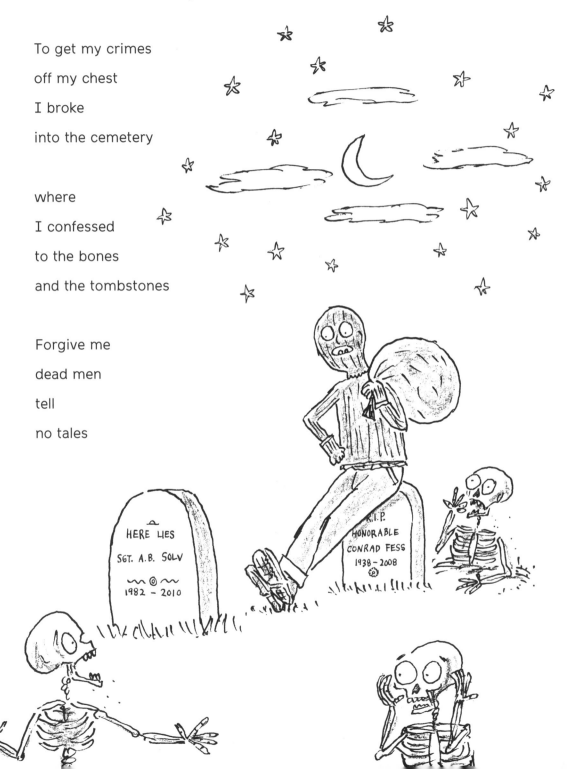

This Is Just to Say

I moved recently

into my new

old

house

through which

you ghoulishly

expected to stump forever

headless and trailing blood

Forgive me

residents

must clean up

after themselves

This Is Just to Say

I have run away

from home

with Muffie

and

they surprisingly

let her

on the plane

Forgive me

we just

landed in—

never mind

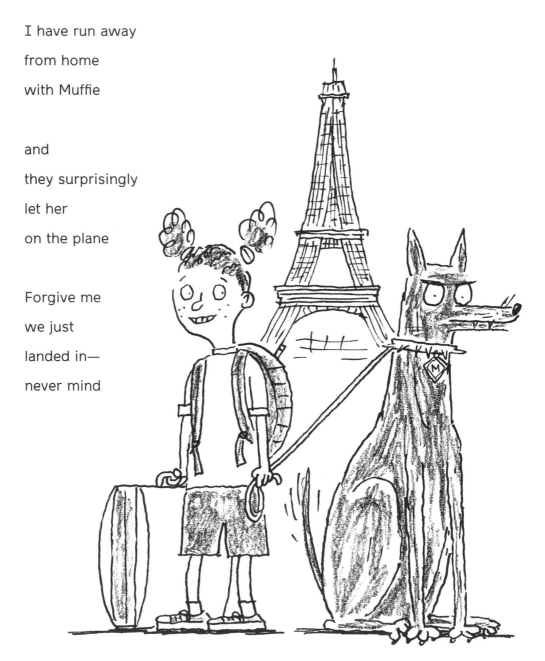

This Is Just to Say

They sing
The bear
went over
the mountain

which
leads him repeatedly
to see
other mountains

Forgive me
no one sings the ending
the landslide
and the dead bear

This Is Just to Say

When you arrive
I will not be
lying
in my bed

where
you hungrily
hoped
to find me

Forgive me
tell my granddaughter
better one of us
should live

This Is Just to Say

I heard
screams
coming from the cottage

which
I should valiantly
and immediately
have entered

Forgive me
at the time
I preferred
to finish my bubble bath

This Is Just to Say

I'm the one
who stuck
the cradle
in the tree

which
was probably
a stupid place
to put a baby

Forgive me
I thought
that bough would break
sooner or later

This Is Just to Say

Last night

I plucked

your baby

from your arms

when

you carelessly

fell

asleep

Forgive me

just guess my assumed name

in the Dwarf

Witness Protection Program

This Is Just to Say

I have sent

a hungry lion

into your parents'

hotel room

just when

they were tenderly

talking about

how wonderful you are

Forgive me

I am

starting

an orphanage

This Is Just to Say

I confess

I sliced off

their skinny

tails

which

they seemed awfully

fond

of waving

Forgive me

I wanted symmetry

sightless in front

tailless behind

This Is Just to Say

I, Rapunzel,
and not the witch

have lopped off

my braid

which

you daily

climbed

to me

Forgive me

you're not worth

the pain

in my scalp

This Is Just to Say

You screamed

while I

yanked out

your hook

which

would doubtlessly

have injured the crocodile

when it ate you

Forgive me

I hate

cruelty

to animals

This Is Just to Say

Soon

you will

visit

your cousins

who thoughtlessly

broke your bicycle

and chewed your gum

last time

Forgive me

you're

staying

a month

This Is Just to Say

It was I

who shoved

you

off the wall

which

you had precariously

perched on

for centuries

Forgive me

all the king's horses

and all the king's men

were bored

This Is Just to Say

By feeling inside

your right snow boot

I located

your diary

which

you moronically

left

where anyone could find it

Forgive me

a year's allowance

and your college fund

will buy my silence

This Is Just to Say

The principal

may mention

my science project

in a phone call

which

could conceivably

threaten expulsion

and marks on my permanent record

Forgive me

I proved my hypothesis

blood is thicker

than water

This Is Just to Say

I gagged
your little brother
and tied him up
at school

after
you clearly
said what a brat
he is

Forgive me
I can't remember
which locker
I stuffed him in

This Is Just to Say

I have torn

down

the water

spout

which

you obsessively

wanted to climb up

and slide off forever

Forgive me

kick your habit

spin a web

catch a bug

This Is Just to Say

From one cup of organic tomatoes

one tarantula

and two tablespoons of ants

I cooked a stew

which

you gluttonously

devoured

then licked the bowl

Forgive me

you are

what

you eat

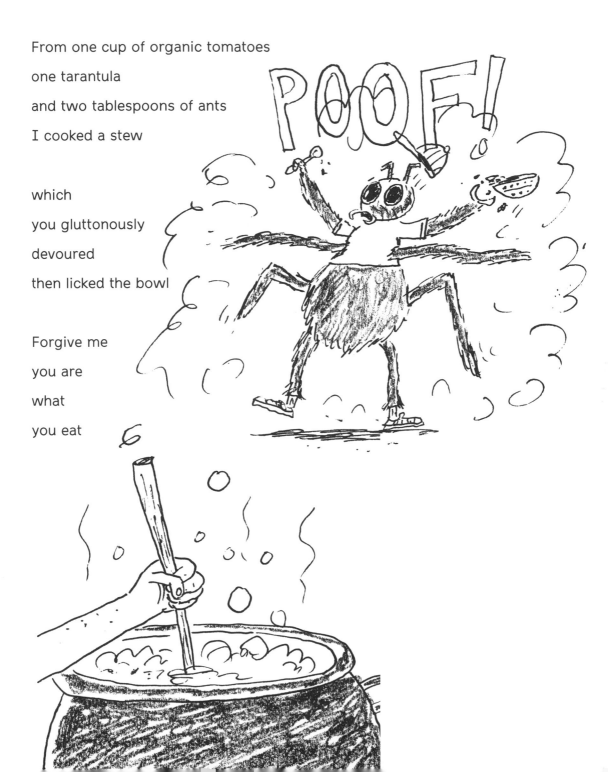

This Is Just to Say

I pushed

your boat

out of the gentle

stream

where

you were merrily

singing

and rowing

Forgive me

life

is but

a nightmare

This Is Just to Say

I already knew

the pea

was under

the mattresses

which

helped immeasurably

in faking

the true princess test

Forgive me

I am a true

evil

enchantress

This Is Just to Say

The moment
it fell off
I snatched
the glass slipper

which
would gloriously
have led you
to Cinderella

Forgive me
I am one-legged
was shoeless
size 3½

This Is Just to Say

I have found

seventeen

cavities

in your teeth

which

you sincerely

wish

were not there

Forgive me

my drill is ready

and I

am in a bad mood

This Is Just to Say

You have reached

the last

of these poems

although

you likely

preferred strep throat

to reading them

Forgive me

I wrote

every one

especially for you